a farm animals' christmas!

no ordinary farm

BY
STEPHANIE MATOLYAK
DEBORAH BAILEY

For the love of all rescued animals
and those who rescue them.

Contributed photography
ℬ BONNIE MCCAFFERY PHOTOGRAPHY | STEPHANIE MATOLYAK | JOSEPH PULICI

BONFIRE MEDIA, LLC
imagination on 🔥

it all started with the first thanksgiving feast on the farm.

the fun times
continue
waiting for
christmas!

time to
have fun in
the snow.

time to decorate for the holidays.

O christmas tree, O christmas tree,
O how we love eating your branches!

time to
go to
bed.

what do you want for christmas?

waiting for the big day to bring...

HEY GANG!!!! ONLY 3 OF US CAN REALLY FLY!!!

WHAT WE NEED IS THE TRACTOR!

WE NEED MORE "REAL" WINGS TO CARRY THIS!!!!

I'M READY FOR A "CAT NAP"!

I SMELL A CARROT!

your christmas wishes!

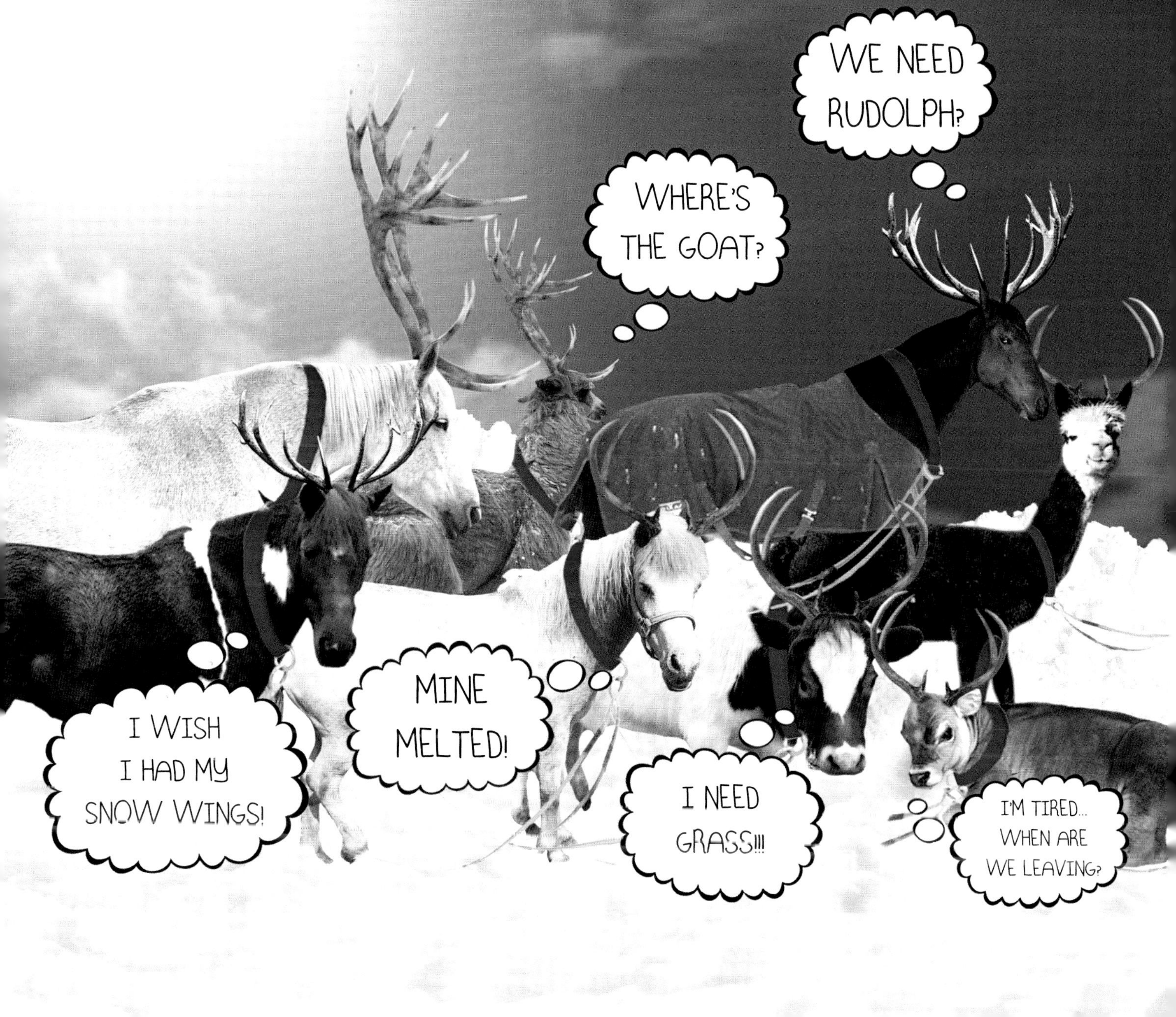

THE REAL STORY

Stephanie's Farm

Once upon a time there was a little girl named Stephanie who loved animals.
She dreamed of living on a farm, but her home was in the city.

Stephanie worked hard in school and got a good job when she grew up.
She saved her money because she never forgot her dream of living on a farm.

One day she went to the veterinarian's office to pick up a new kitten she had adopted.
In the waiting room she saw a book that had farms for sale.
She opened it and there was the farm of her dreams!

Stephanie went to see the farm. The minute she saw it she knew it was the farm for her!

The farm that nobody wanted now started filling up with animals that nobody wanted.
Stephanie gave these unwanted animals a loving home and now they have lots of fun.

Stephanie's Farm is truly no ordinary farm.
Children and animals have a magical experience together.

Dreams do come true! Do you have a dream?

Thank you for celebrating the holidays on the farm with us!

Here are our names. Want to have more fun? Go back through our story and find us.

"NORM" "MOO" "FRANKIE" "NIKI" "JULIET"

"SCARLET" "RHET" "JELLYBEAN" "MIMI" "ABBY"

"CHEEPY" "MOE" "RED" "GOLDIE" "LESTER"

"HENRY" "SNOWFLAKE" "GINNY" "JACK" "JILL"

"LOKI" "DUSTY" "AMIGO" "ARIES" "RICKI"

"ANGEL" "TOPPO" "DIRTYBOOTS" "MOUSE" "FLY"

We look forward to introducing you to even more of us in our next adventure.

WORKING TOGETHER

STEPHANIE MATOLYAK

DEBORAH BAILEY

Stephanie is a top rated Realtor in northeastern PA. For many years she has been living her dream on a farm in the country. She brings her "Personal Touch" to her real estate business by creating an annual Christmas card based on her farm which all of her clients look forward to every year. *"a farm animals' christmas!-no ordinary farm"* is a culmination of these Christmas card masterpieces over the years.

Her clients, their families and friends enjoy visits to Stephanie's Farm, interacting with a large assortment of animals that Stephanie has rescued. Real Estate and animals are her passion and they both flourish in this amazingly beautiful northeastern, PA environment.

Originally from Johnstown, PA, Stephanie grew up as a competitive gymnast. She then moved to New York City to pursue her study of dance, acting and the big stage! The new aerobic dance craze took Stephanie to Italy, opening aerobic studios throughout Italy. Upon returning to NYC, Stephanie worked with developers designing and managing private health clubs in the new high-rise condominium buildings.

As a business owner of "Spa Finders" came an exciting career in the health spa industry, publishing a magazine and setting up spa networks around the world.

Throughout her different careers, Stephanie enjoyed investing in real estate. Among one of her purchases was her farm in NE PA which she used as a weekend getaway from Manhattan. Soon it became harder to leave this paradise to go back to the city, thus she stayed and started her very successful real estate career and the procession of rescued animals.

Deborah, the creative artist behind Stephanie's Christmas card masterpieces and *"a farm animals' christmas!-no ordinary farm"* magical picture book, has spent her entire career in the graphic design and sales arena. She is the owner of Bailey Design and Advertising, a twenty year old award winning boutique graphic design and advertising agency. She also owns and publishes Connections Magazine, a Pocono Mountain favorite entertainment and recreation magazine, established in 1998.

Deborah grew up in beautiful historic Honesdale, Wayne County, PA and still resides here with her family. She is a proud mother of three daughters and grandmother. She enjoys oil painting, gardening, hiking, biking, and kayaking with her little yaker doggie, Petey, a Chiweenie, who she rescued in 2016.

Deborah has sat on many business and non-profit organizational boards throughout her career, currently sits on the Board of Trustees of Lackawanna College, and volunteers in her community.

Deborah and Bailey Design and Advertising have received many awards and honors over the years. Vision of Advocacy Award from Safe Haven of Pike County, PA, America's Registry of Outstanding Professionals, Top 25 Business Women in Northeast PA, a finalist in the nation for Enterprising Women in business, Small Business Administration (SBA) Northeastern Pennsylvania Woman Entrepreneur designation, and recipient of numerous Communicator Awards of Distinction for graphic design.

Deborah's motto in life is to go forward in the face of overwhelming odds even if it means risking failure. Risks must be taken, because the greatest hazard in life is to risk nothing. The person that risks nothing, is nothing.

STEPHANIE AND NORM ON THE FARM!

From all of us on the farm,

Happy New Year!

Stay in touch on facebook

@bonfiremediausa